TRUTH ON TRIAL

TRUTH ON TRIAL
The Story of Galileo Galilei

by Vicki Cobb
illustrated by George Ulrich

COWARD, McCANN & GEOGHEGAN, INC. · NEW YORK

For Eleanor Zabb, my sister

LIBRARY OF CONGRESS CATALOGING IN PUBLICATION DATA
Cobb, Vicki.
Truth on trial.
Bibliography: p.
SUMMARY: A biography of the 16th-century Italian
mathematician, physicist, and astronomer who questioned
the accepted scientific theories of his time and was
tried by the Inquisition for his ideas.
1. Galilei, Galileo, 1564–1642—Juvenile literature.
2. Astronomers—Italy—Biography—Juvenile literature.
[1. Galilei, Galileo, 1564–1642. 2. Scientists]
I. Ulrich, George. II. Title.
QB36.G2C65 1979   520'.92'4 [B] [92]   79-237
ISBN 0-698-30709-7
Printed in the United States of America

CONTENTS

1
Mathematics, Music, and Motion

Florence, 1577

The argument at the end of the great room was getting louder. As the men's voices rose, the candle flickered, casting angry shadows on the high ceiling and marble floor. The subject of this heated discussion was music.

"Look, Vincenzo," Count Bardi was saying. "I don't care what you think. Mathematics and music are related. Surely you agree with Zarlino. After all, he *is* your music teacher. And he's the most respected authority on the subject!"

"I know, I know," Vincenzo Galilei said impatiently. "Don't you think I've studied his book? Page by page, at that. I deeply admire the man!" Abruptly he brought his fist down on the table and leaned toward the Count.

"That's the trouble. I respect him too much. But listen, Bardi. I've composed music according to Zarlino's formulas. I've experimented with his mathematics in my music. All you have to do is listen to it. Frankly, it's terrible! Zarlino's ideas are great on paper but the truth comes out when you hear them as music."

The sound of his father's fist woke thirteen-year-old Galileo Galilei. For a minute he didn't know where he was. Then he remembered. He had come with his father to Count Bardi's home. Like many wealthy noblemen of Italy in the sixteenth century the Count was interested in the arts. He was a musician and had formed a society of musicians. They had regular meetings at his home where they played and discussed the modern music of their time. Galileo's father, Vincenzo, was a fine musician and composer. The lute was his main instrument and he could also play the organ. He had taught his son to play both instruments, and Galileo was already a good musician.

Galileo sometimes went with his father to Count Bardi's meetings. He loved being included in the men's world of music and talk. But this night was later than usual. The others had already left and his father and the Count had fallen into their habit of arguing. Galileo had not been able to keep his eyes open and had fallen asleep.

Galileo coughed. Count Bardi seemed relieved at the interruption.

"It's late, Vincenzo," he said gently. "There's no point arguing about what's good in music. People have different tastes. So you experimented and, in your view, you failed. I'll bet I can compose something using Zarlino's rules that will impress you. At least, no one will fall asleep when I play it." He winked at Galileo.

Vincenzo turned toward his son.

"I'm sorry, Galileo," he said. "I didn't realize it was so late. I lose all sense of time when the Count and I get going. Help me pack up and let's go home."

Galileo was glad his father and the Count could argue and still remain friends. He would hate to think they could have a falling out that could end these visits. Galileo enjoyed the Count's home, especially this room. He looked up at the magnificent paintings that hung from the high carved ceiling. The city of Florence was famous for its painting and sculpture. Every wealthy nobleman had an art collection and Count Bardi was no exception. Buying art was one of the main ways the noble classes helped artists earn a living.

Galileo's family was well-born, but far from wealthy. Vincenzo made most of his living as a cloth merchant. Yet he made sure Galileo and his other children learned the skills of music and art that wealthy children learned. Galileo was talented in everything he did. He was a joy to teach and learned with every experience.

Vincenzo carefully placed his lute in its case. Galileo picked up his father's music. As they were about to leave, the Count rose to his feet.

"Vincenzo, Galileo, let's not end the evening on a sour note. You may be right, Vincenzo. After all, you've actually experimented. For you, composing with mathematics doesn't work. Why don't you write your teacher and tell him you think he's wrong?"

"I've been thinking about that, my dear Count," said Vincenzo. "But you know how difficult it is to go against authority. Zarlino is famous. He won't like having his ideas challenged. But I know the truth. I'm thinking of writing a book that will prove he's wrong."

Galileo looked at his father with admiration. It took courage to challenge the ideas of the powerful. Galileo didn't know it then, but someday he would be doing the same thing, only on a much more important matter. He would someday challenge the authority of the greatest power in all of Italy, the Church of Rome. But on this night he knew nothing of his future. He only knew he had slept through something interesting, something about mathematics . . . his favorite subject.

"Papa, what's all this about mathematics and music?" Galileo asked as soon as the Count's door had closed behind them.

"Well, Galileo, you know when you play the lute you make different notes by pressing on the strings. This changes the length of the strings. An Egyptian astronomer named Ptolemy measured the length of the strings that produced certain notes and said the most beautiful music would be made by strings with certain measurements. My teacher agrees. But when I composed with these notes it sounded terrible."

Galileo had learned about Ptolemy, and he remembered that Ptolemy had also used numbers to explain the motion of heavenly bodies. Galileo looked up at the starry night sky and asked, "Papa, how does the universe work?"

Vincenzo smiled in the darkness. He was used to his son's quick mind and what seemed to be its changes of subject. He knew Ptolemy's name had started Galileo thinking about the universe, and how mathematics might fit into it.

"People have always noticed that heavenly bodies move across the sky," Vincenzo replied. "The first person who tried to explain the motion in the universe was Aristotle."

Galileo also knew about Aristotle. He was a famous Greek thinker who had lived about 2,000 years before. He had investigated all kinds of subjects and had written down his explanations for everything he had

observed. Aristotle's work was rediscovered in Europe more than 1,000 years later and was considered to be the beginning of modern thought. In Galileo's time people believed that he knew just about everything about the natural world anyone could know. Other thinkers, like Ptolemy, who came later, did not change Aristotle's basic ideas. They just added details and filled in facts. Aristotle's teachings were one of the main subjects in Galileo's school.

"What do people believe about the universe today?" asked Galileo.

Father and son walked in comfortable silence as Vincenzo gathered his thoughts.

"The universe is made up of the earth and all the heavenly bodies," Vincenzo began slowly. "There are different kinds of heavenly bodies: the sun, moon, stars, and planets. They are all perfect and never change. The earth, on the other hand, is not perfect. It's always changing with seasons, volcanos, storms, and winds. But the earth is the home of man, God's greatest creation. For this reason, it occupies the most important place in the universe, the very center. All the heavenly bodies move in perfect circles around the earth.

"Ptolemy figured out how the universe is arranged. He made many measurements of the positions of the heavenly bodies as they moved across the sky. Each object is attached to an invisible crystal globe that keeps it from falling onto the earth. The globes are inside each other, like the layers of an onion, and each globe has its own motion, which we see as the bodies move across the sky. The closest globe is the one that holds up the moon. Just outside this is the globe that belongs to the planet Mercury. Next is Venus. Then the one that holds the sun. The

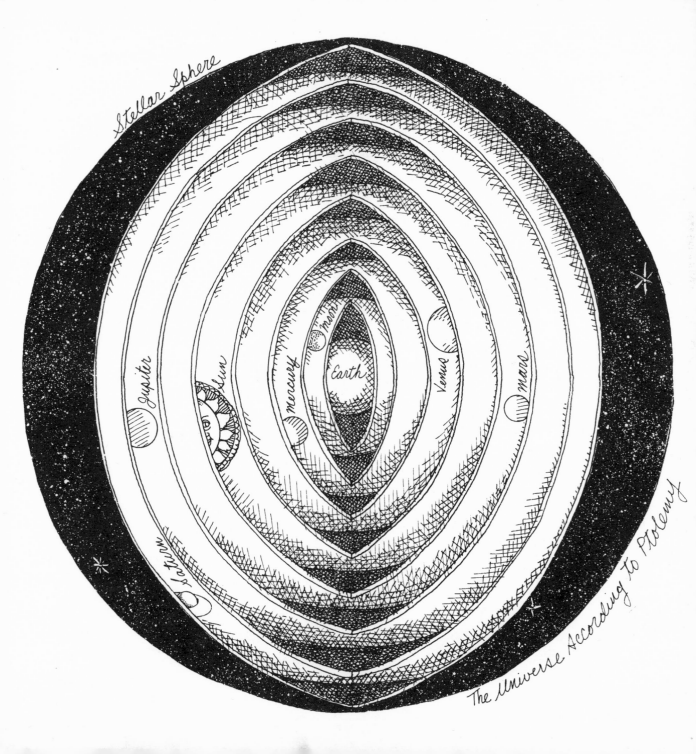

Stellar Sphere

Jupiter

Saturn

Sun

Mercury

Moon

Earth

Venus

Mars

The Universe According To Ptolemy

planets Mars, Jupiter, and Saturn each have their transparent globes, and farthest away is the one that holds all the stars."

"The order of the heavens is beautiful," said Galileo.

"Yes. Ptolemy believed such order made for harmony in the heavens. Just like good music."

Their steps had slowed. They were nearing home, and both father and son wanted to delay going in. They sat down on some nearby church steps.

"Galileo, it's time we talked about how you'll earn a living."

"Mama wants me to be a cloth merchant, like you," said Galileo.

"You are too gifted for that, my son. We must find another way," answered Vincenzo.

"The brothers who teach me at the monastery think I am good in mathematics and in my studies," said Galileo.

"Mathematicians don't earn anything. All they can do is be professors. No—I would like you to go to the university. There you will become a doctor. That profession pays well."

Vincenzo stood up. He put his arm around his son's shoulders as they walked toward their home. "Yes, keep up your studies and I will make sure you can go to the university. Your career as a physician will bring honor and wealth to the Galilei family."

2

A Challenging Talk, A Daring Thought

Padua, 1598

The lecture hall was packed, as usual. The students were watching intently, completely caught up in the magic of the lesson. On the platform at the end of the room was a stocky young professor with a reddish beard named Galileo Galilei. Galileo had followed his father's wishes and gone to the university in Pisa, where he had started on a program in medicine. Soon, however, his first love, mathematics, took over. When he graduated, he took a job teaching mathematics in Pisa. It paid poorly as his father had predicted. That had been especially hard on his family. His father had died seven years before, and they were short on money. But for the past six years he had been teaching here in Padua, in the Republic of Venice, 150 miles from home, and this position had been good for him. He was still not paid very well, but there was an air of freedom in Padua, and Galileo had blossomed as a daring and original thinker and a first-rate teacher.

In the seventeenth century, Italy was not one nation as it is now, but rather was divided into many small states. Some, like the Republic of

Venice, were under control of the people who lived there. Such local control encouraged free thinking. Other states, like Tuscany, where Galileo had grown up, were under control of the Church of Rome, so that the Pope was the head of the government as well as the Church. The Church was powerful enough to smother ideas it disagreed with.

As he spoke in the lecture hall, Galileo was obviously enjoying his ideas. Although he had not become a doctor, his father would have been proud of him. His lectures had a very strong effect on students, and it was easy to see why. Galileo talked as if he were looking for an argument. Very few students were willing to take him on. The ones who did took their chances, since Galileo had a way of tripping up even careful and intelligent speakers.

Galileo was weaving a spell over his audience. His eyes glittered as he paced back and forth.

"Let me tell you what happened to me when I was a student at Pisa. I was looking at something all of you have seen hundreds of times in your lives—but I'm sure none of you noticed what I did."

Everyone was caught up in the excitement of Galileo's thinking.

"I was in church," Galileo was saying. "An overhead lamp had just been lit. The lamplighter had set it in motion and it was swinging back and forth." Galileo put his hands on his hips and faced the group squarely. "Now let's do some hard thinking about the motion of a swinging lamp. How would you describe it?" Silence. Galileo let his piercing eyes search around the room for some poor volunteer.

Today no one dared answer, so the professor answered his own question. "A swinging lamp is a pendulum. It cuts an arc as it moves back and forth. After a while the arc gets smaller and smaller until the pendulum comes to rest. Sometimes this takes a long time." Again Galileo challenged his students.

"At first, the pendulum cuts a wide arc. Eventually it cuts a small one. Which arc takes longer?" Galileo waited. At first no one answered. Then a few students called out.

"The long path."

"It takes longer to make a big arc."

Galileo smiled. He knew he had them in the palm of his hand.

"But a pendulum is moving faster when it is cutting a long arc," he responded.

Some students reconsidered their answer.

"Then it must take longer to make a small arc."

The professor shook his finger at his class.

"You don't know the answer, do you? If you learn nothing else from me, never be ashamed of not knowing! I know I've asked what seems to be a simple question. I found the truth by experimenting. I watched the lamp. Suddenly I realized that the swings could be timed by my pulse, since it has a regular beat. So I put my fingers on my wrist and counted, and I found that the long swings took *exactly* as much time as the short ones.

"Here, I'll show you." Galileo took two lengths of chain from behind his desk. A small iron ball hung from the end of each chain.

"You will notice that these chains are the same length and the bobs are exactly the same weight."

He hung the chains on two pegs sticking out of a beam on the wall behind him.

"I want all the students on the left side of the room to clap to the beat of this pendulum." Galileo drew one of the pendulums aside so it was completely horizontal. He let it drop so it swung back and forth in a wide arc. Then he gently pushed the other pendulum to set it moving in a small arc. He signaled the other half of the room to clap to the beat of its small swing. The sound grew strong. Suddenly everyone realized that the entire room was clapping in a steady beat together! Galileo's experiment revealed the truth. The size of the swing of a pendulum did not affect the time it took to make it.

Galileo raised his hands. The clapping stopped.

"Gentlemen, my point is made."

This time the hands joined in a round of applause. The lesson for the day was over. Galileo waited patiently for the room to clear. When he looked up, he saw his favorite former student, Sagredo, leaning against the wall, watching him.

"Sagredo, you devil! What are you doing here?" Galileo rushed forward to greet his friend.

"I'm in Padua for a few days on business and I thought I'd drop by. I see you're still using your old material."

"Listen, my friend. Some ideas get better with time," laughed Galileo. "But it is good to see you. So you think I have nothing new to say? Come home with me to dinner. We'll see if there is nothing new to discuss."

20

Sagredo accepted with pleasure. He had many fond memories of good food, wine, and talk at his old teacher's home.

This night proved to be no exception. Several of Galileo's students boarded at his house, as Sagredo had done in his student days. The university didn't pay enough for Galileo to make ends meet, so he opened his home to boarders. Dinner conversation was lively. Sagredo told stories of his wild student days and some of the fun he and Galileo had. One thing was certain. Galileo was not a stuffy professor. He liked good times like most young men.

After dinner, Sagredo and Galileo went into his study.

"So, my friend," said Sagredo, "what's the cause of your new excitement?"

"This book," said Galileo, picking up a heavy leather-bound volume. "It's more than fifty years old. It was written by a Polish churchman named Nicolaus Copernicus. He spent his life studying the heavens and put all his findings in this book. What he says about the universe goes against everything the scholars at the universities and the Church of Rome state as the truth. I discovered it in my early student days and have been thinking about it for a long time."

"Are you telling me," Sagredo said slowly, "that you believe in this book and that you are going to do something so others will believe it also?"

"You know me too well, Sagredo. There is no question that people are afraid of the new ideas in this book. Even Copernicus knew his truth would stir people up. He was afraid to have his book published. Look, in the introduction he says, 'I feared I would be laughed off the stage.'

He even dedicated the book to the Pope, hoping the Pope wouldn't ban the book. And he waited until he was an old man before he gave his book to the printer. Imagine! He first saw his book on his deathbed."

"What are his ideas, anyway, that they can make the Church so angry?" asked Sagredo.

"Well, you know we all teach about the universe the way Aristotle and Ptolemy did. The earth is at the center and the sun, moon, planets, and stars all move in crystal balls around us. Copernicus dares to say that the *sun*, not the earth, is at the center. And the earth is just another planet. Look, here he says the earth is moving: 'In the middle of all sits the sun, like a king. From here he can light all the planets at once. The sun sits as if on a throne ruling his children, the planets which circle him.' "

"How do you know that his system is the truth?" asked Sagredo. "After all, the evidence is that the heavenly bodies move around us. You can *see* that happening."

"You always were one of my best students, Sagredo. The fact is that there is no proof that Copernicus is right! I just have a hunch he is. For one thing, his system is much simpler than Ptolemy's. You know the paths of the planets are not simple like the sun, moon, and stars. Planets sometimes have a backward motion. Under the present system we add extra circles to the planetary motions so that their paths look like curlicues. Copernicus gets rid of the curlicues and makes their paths simple circles again. He can do this because he says the earth is *passing* another planet as they both move around the sun. This makes the other planet *seem* to be moving backward. All the planets are moving in the

same direction in circular paths around the sun, including earth."

"What about the path of the sun across the sky in the daytime and the paths of the moon and stars at night?" asked Sagredo.

"Copernicus says the earth has two ways of moving. It spins like a top while it moves around the sun. It is this spinning motion that makes the sun appear to move across the sky by day and the moon and stars *appear* to move across the sky at night. Actually we are the ones who move, though we feel no motion. I tell you, Sagredo," Galileo added with feeling, "the man is right. His system is beautifully simple. And it's based on more than thirty years of carefully tracking the paths of all the heavenly bodies."

"Then why isn't it accepted? Why aren't people arguing over it?"

"First, as I said, there is no proof Copernicus is correct. Right now, it's only his opinion. Secondly, his book is hard to read. It requires careful study. It's not widely known, so it's not yet a threat to the Church. But mark my words, my friend. Someday soon there will be proof Copernicus is right. And I will not be shy about speaking out. You can count on that!"

Sagredo glanced out the window into the night. Venus, called the evening star, was rising in the east. Perhaps Galileo's star was rising, too.

3

Letters, Discoveries, Messages

Padua, 1610

Galileo's hands trembled with anticipation as he opened the long-awaited letter. He read it quickly, then sighed with relief. After eighteen years of hard work in Padua, Galileo could finally go home to his beloved country of Tuscany. The Grand Duke Cosimo, his former student, asked him to be chief mathematician and philosopher of the court in Florence. The Duke would match the good salary Galileo was now receiving. And what was more, Galileo wouldn't have to teach. He could spend all his time doing what he wanted—experimenting and writing. It was a dream come true—not that he wouldn't miss his friends in the Venetian Republic, and the freedom he had had to develop his ideas, even unpopular ones.

Galileo sat down on a bench in his garden and thought how the past year had been filled with discovery and adventure.

The previous summer, in 1609, Galileo had been visiting friends in Venice. One of them told him about an invention of Hans Lippershey, a Dutch lens grinder, that made it possible to see distant objects as if they were much closer. This "spyglass" had become a fad among the royalty of Europe, who thought of it as a clever toy. It wasn't much good for anything but fun, since the image was fuzzy and upside down.

But Galileo was fascinated by the invention. When he got home he figured out a way to make a similar instrument. He ground two lenses in his workshop and mounted them at either end of a tube made of lead. When he looked through it, he saw objects as if they were three times closer and about ten times larger than they appeared to the naked eye. They were also right side up. Excited with his success, Galileo set about making another instrument. It was a big improvement over the first, bringing objects eight times closer.

In August, Galileo made a present of a telescope (as his instrument had been named) to the head of the Venetian Republic. The presentation was made in a public ceremony before hundreds of people. Officials of the government climbed a tower used to watch for approaching ships. They were amazed to find that Galileo's telescope made it possible to see a ship more than two hours before it could be seen with the naked eye, and they immediately saw how important the telescope could be in warfare—war was always a possibility among the small Italian states.

Galileo was handsomely rewarded for his invention. He was given an enormous raise in salary and a lifetime position at the university. Orders for telescopes came pouring in. Galileo got better and better at grinding lenses and kept his methods secret so no one could make a better telescope. He kept his best one for himself. It enlarged objects almost 1,000 times and brought them thirty-three times closer. And while others turned their telescopes on earthly objects, Galileo took his

telescope to the top of a tower and turned it toward the night sky.

Imagine having the power to see farther than anyone had ever seen! Where to look first? Galileo chose the moon, which people then thought to be a perfectly polished sphere. To Galileo's astonishment he saw it was not smooth at all, but had mountains and valleys and craters, like the earth. Sunlight made the mountains cast giant shadows, and Galileo used mathematics to calculate the height of the mountains from their shadows. They were the same size as some mountains on earth! Knowing the size of the mountains made them seem that much more real. This discovery was overwhelming. In one glance through the telescope an old idea was destroyed. At least one heavenly body was not perfect!

Next, Galileo turned his telescope toward the stars. Again surprises were in store for him. The Milky Way had always been a mystery. To the naked eye it appears to be a faintly glowing band of light stretching across the sky. But now Galileo saw that it was made up of countless stars arranged in clusters. No matter where he pointed the telescope, a vast crowd of stars immediately came into view. The telescope certainly showed the limits of human eyesight. Nature contained far more than anyone had ever seen before.

On a clear winter night in January he made his greatest discovery of all. He looked at the planet Jupiter. Next to the planet were three points of light which appeared to be stars. Since Galileo was seeing new stars every night, he might easily have ignored these near Jupiter, except for one strange thing: the three "starlets" were arranged in a row that was even with the equator of the planet. He made a sketch in his notebook:

The next night, when he looked at Jupiter, this is what he saw:

How could Jupiter be east of all three "starlets" when the night before it had been west of two of them? Obviously something was moving, but what? And how? Galileo could hardly wait for the next night. Unfortunately it was clouded over, so he had to wait two nights. This time there were only two "starlets," and they were back on the east side of the planet:

There had to be an explanation. Nothing like this had ever been known, or even imagined, as far as Galileo knew. Jupiter's motion was very well known. Astronomers had been mapping its path for centuries. There was no way that the change in the positions of the "starlets" could be caused by the movement of Jupiter. Galileo concluded that these tiny bright bodies must have a motion all their own.

After the fourth night of observation, Galileo was certain he knew what was happening. He was sure he had seen three heavenly bodies revolving around Jupiter.

For the next month Galileo studied the planet and discovered a fourth "starlet" revolving around Jupiter. Now he had seen with his own eyes four heavenly bodies circling another planet. This disproved the Church of Rome's teaching that all heavenly bodies revolved around the earth. It was also a proof of the Copernican system: if these "starlets" could move around a planet, the planets themselves could move round the sun.

Galileo knew that the Church would disapprove of any evidence against its position. His new knowledge could be dangerous and even his personal safety might depend on his keeping it a secret. Despite the risk, however, he couldn't resist sharing his newly found truths with the world. He quickly wrote a slim book called *A Messenger from the Stars*. It contained all his discoveries and was published in March 1610, only ten days after his last recorded look at Jupiter. There were some people who would later say that Galileo wrote the book as if he, himself, were the messenger from the heavens, and there were many who took offense

34

at Galileo's immodest claims on behalf of the truth of his observations.

But Galileo felt only joy at making his discoveries public. He decided to use this book to honor the man he hoped would support him, the Grand Duke of Tuscany. Not only did he dedicate the book to the Grand Duke, but he named the four moons of Jupiter the "Medicean stars" after the Grand Duke's family name of Medici. No other ruler on earth had heavenly bodies named after him. The Grand Duke surely could not ignore such a tribute.

Today, in the hot June sun, as he looked at the letter in his hand, Galileo saw his plan had worked. The Grand Duke had offered him a position at his court.

Galileo allowed himself to dream about his new life. He would have the support of his former student, the head of the Tuscan government, who would allow him to do as he wished. He wouldn't be bothered with money matters or teaching duties. He would be free, freer than ever, to see his family, to walk in the countryside of his childhood, and best of all, to write his book comparing the two systems of the universe. He would show the world that Copernicus, not Ptolemy, was right.

Galileo had no idea how false his sense of security was.

4
A Trip to Rome
1615-1616

Galileo appeared to have no second thoughts about leaving Padua, but many people were upset by his move. The university officials had only recently doubled his salary and given him a lifetime position, and they took Galileo's leaving as an insult. Some of Galileo's friends questioned the wisdom of his action. One friend wrote:

"Where will you find the same liberty as here in the Venetian Republic? Here you had support and protection, especially as your friends grew more and more powerful. Here you were free to have unpopular ideas, to serve only yourself. Now you serve your Grand Duke, who is a good man. But in a court there can be envious men who can make even a good ruler ruin an honest man such as yourself. I am especially worried by your being in a place where the power of the Grand Duke can be overruled by the Church of Rome."

Galileo at first thought little of political dangers. He never wanted to think of the Church of Rome as his enemy, since he deeply loved Catholicism. But the Church's double role could cause conflicts. In Tuscany the head of state was tied to the political as well as spiritual side of the Church, and the Church was extremely powerful. The government in the Venetian Republic was free of the Church's political power. There, an individual could oppose the Church safely. But in Tuscany threatening ideas would not go unnoticed.

Galileo made this unhappy discovery shortly after moving back to Florence, when he received an ominous note from an artist friend in Rome. It warned of a plot to have a priest denounce Galileo's work from the pulpit and to condemn the teaching of mathematics.

As much as Galileo might have wished everyone to be good, to want to know the truth, in real life it was not possible. Galileo was soon to be exposed to what he called the greatest hatred of all—the hatred ignorance has for knowledge. He couldn't believe that he was unable to convince everyone of the truth, and so he set about trying. Unfortunately, his earnest outspokenness backfired and made him even more enemies.

The problem was that Galileo's discoveries seemed to disagree with the Bible. Galileo, a religious man and a good Catholic, saw no conflict between the Copernican system of the universe and the scriptures. He felt that the words of the Bible could not always be taken at face value, but that they should be interpreted to find spiritual truth. For him the Bible had little bearing on scientific truth, and he was fond of saying, "The Bible shows the way to go to heaven, not the way the heavens go."

However, churchmen who made the interpretation of the Bible their profession disagreed. Who was Galileo, a philosopher and scientist, to preach on the meaning of holy writings?

In 1615, pressures on Galileo began to build. Just as his artist friend had warned, a powerful priest publicly condemned the teaching of mathematics and the Copernican system. He suggested that both subjects be banned from the universities. Galileo's friends were afraid for him. One friend urged him to be silent and let the problem go away.

"But if I do nothing, doesn't it prove my enemies are right? I can't let them have the last word," retorted Galileo.

His friends often reminded him of an incident that had occurred fifteen years before. A philosopher named Giordano Bruno had published a book on the nature of the universe. He had scorned many traditional ideas and made many statements that disagreed with Church positions, including statements in favor of the Copernican system. As a result he was imprisoned by the Inquisition, the powerful court of the Church that was supposed to protect its doctrines. Bruno was found guilty of opposing God and the Church, and he was burned at the stake. His fate showed what could happen to Galileo.

Nevertheless, Galileo was not deterred.

"The Inquisition has not summoned me or condemned me yet," Galileo said. "Perhaps it has changed in fifteen years. I will make the first move and volunteer to talk to the powers in Rome. When they hear the logic of my arguments they will see the correctness of the Copernican system and that it is no threat to Catholicism. I cannot let Copernicus be condemned. His work is too important to the world."

On December 3, 1615, Galileo set off for Rome. He already had the support of powerful friends. Now he hoped to convince the Pope's

Secretary of State, Cardinal Bellarmine, of his cause. Bellarmine had a reputation for being an intelligent and fair man, and he was as close to the Pope as it was possible to be. Bellarmine might influence the Holy Father in Galileo's favor, so Galileo could sidestep the Inquisition altogether. Galileo was confident in the truth as revealed by his scientific method and in his ability to convince people to see things his way. After all, he had convinced hundreds of students. Why should Church rulers in Rome be more difficult?

Galileo arrived in Rome two days later and stayed in great comfort at the palace of the Tuscan ambassador. The two had long talks about the Church's strength in Europe. For a century, new Protestant churches in other parts of Europe had severely challenged the Church's power and the Church had lost some of the wide-ranging influence it had traditionally enjoyed. Europe had often been at war over questions of religion, and some of the Protestant countries, like England, were very powerful.

Galileo's appearance in Rome caught Church officials by surprise. He found it would be weeks before he could meet with Bellarmine, and since he could not yet speak directly to Church officials, he spent his time making his views known at one party after another.

"Rome is certainly changing for the better," Galileo thought to himself as he rode through the streets on his way to a dinner at the home of a cardinal. Everywhere there was construction. Old, crowded buildings were being torn down and replaced with huge squares and avenues, magnificent palaces, splashing fountains, and splendid sculptures. "Perhaps people are ready to change their thinking along

with their architecture," Galileo mused. Deep down, however, he wasn't sure. The waiting was taking its toll and he worried that his views were being discussed unfavorably by high Church officials.

As usual, Galileo had brought his telescope with him this evening. He loved giving everyone a chance to see the Medicean stars, the landscape on the moon, and the thousands of stars invisible to the naked eye. And, as usual, he was the center of attention. He handled the guests' questions in a well-practiced manner.

"How do you know that the Medicean stars aren't in the lens of the telescope?" asked one disbeliever at the cardinal's dinner.

"If they were, you'd see them no matter where you pointed the instrument," Galileo answered.

"How do your discoveries prove that the sun is the center of the universe? Why are you disregarding Aristotle and Ptolemy?" asked another.

Galileo took a deep breath, winding up for his standard lecture on the subject. But before he could say a word a deep voice boomed, "The old theory of Ptolemy simply made mathematical order out of the heavens. It has become harder to use it and it has grown extremely complicated as more facts have been observed by astronomers." Galileo turned and saw the imposing figure of Cardinal Maffeo Barberini, who was one of the few truly gifted men of science in Rome. "Galileo's discoveries are evidence in favor of Copernicus's plan, which is simpler mathematically," continued the Cardinal.

Galileo was grateful: at last, a guest who understood. So often it seemed as if people looked on him as entertainment. They listened, they nodded and smiled, and they forgot. They didn't seem to realize the serious nature of his arguments. But Cardinal Barberini was different. Galileo had enjoyed long discussions with him on his last visit to Rome four years ago.

"Tell me, Galileo," said Cardinal Barberini, "Do you think that the Copernican system is true? Are the planets—including the earth—really moving around the sun? Or is it just a way of thinking about what we observe?"

"I believe Copernicus is right," answered Galileo. "Very often what we see as 'real' is not what is actually happening. I have been studying nature just for the purpose of finding out what is true in it. And I have discovered over and over again that while we humans can be mistaken, nature never lies."

The Cardinal's eyes began to sparkle. He liked nothing better than a challenging talk with a great mind like Galileo's.

"Let's get away from the heavens, for a moment. What have your studies shown about earthly matters?"

"Well," answered Galileo thoughtfully, "this may be hard for you to believe, but I swear it's the truth: a ball rolling along a level surface should never stop. It should roll forever."

Cardinal Barberini laughed. "Now I've heard everything! First you want to move the earth. Now you say balls should roll forever. Everyone knows that all rolling balls come to a stop sooner or later."

"Ah, that's true. But when you look closer, if you do what I call a 'thought experiment,' you'll see that a rolling ball should keep rolling. Here, follow my reasoning. Tell me, how does a ball roll down a hill?"

"What a simple question," commented the Cardinal. "Obviously, it rolls faster and faster."

"Yes, it picks up speed. Now tell me, how does a ball roll after you give it a shove up a hill?"

Cardinal Barberini began to see the logic behind Galileo's thinking. "It rolls more and more slowly until it stops for an instant and rolls back down the hill."

"Yes. And now comes the only possible conclusion. If a ball picks up speed as it rolls down a hill, and loses speed as it rolls up a hill, how *should* it roll on a level surface?"

"You are a genius!" exclaimed Cardinal Barberini. "A ball on a level surface, where this is no hill, should not speed up or slow down. It should roll at the same speed forever! How do you explain the fact that all balls do finally stop rolling?"

"Obviously, something is slowing them down—something to do with the contact between the surfaces. One day I will write a book on questions like this. I'll write it after my book comparing the two systems of the universe."

"I understand you are waiting to see Cardinal Bellarmine. I wish you luck. I have a hunch, my friend, that you would do better to stick to your new studies and drop this issue of Copernicus."

Galileo remained deaf to all such warnings. Perhaps he had heard too many of them. He was here in Rome. He would see Cardinal Bellarmine, and he would convince him and the other disbelievers.

At last, near the end of February, Galileo had his long-awaited meeting with Cardinal Bellarmine. It did not go as he had hoped.

Some Church officials had met earlier in the month. They had summed up Galileo's beliefs about the universe in two statements:

1. The sun is the center of the universe and does not move.
2. The earth is not the center of the universe. It moves around the sun and also spins to make night and day.

This summary had been given to the Inquisition, which advised the Pope that Galileo's thinking was dangerous.

Galileo never had a chance to present his case when he met with Bellarmine. A decision about him had already been made, and Bellarmine was now simply following the Pope's orders.

"Galileo," Bellarmine said as kindly as possible, "it is my duty to warn you that you must not hold or defend the Copernican system of the universe."

Galileo fully understood what was behind the Cardinal's words. To the Church he was a threat, and so he must be silenced.

Three days after the Cardinal's warning, Copernicus's treatise was put on the Church's list of forbidden books.

Words of the action against Galileo spread quickly through Rome. Since people respected him, they treated him with kindness. Though in public he appeared to accept the Church's orders, his best friends knew that his spirit was not broken.

Galileo was now fifty-two years old. He would have to wait for a while and be silent. But someday his ideas would be published. Galileo was not the type to give up his battle against ignorance.

46

5

The Trial

Florence and Rome, 1632–1633

Galileo walked stiffly into the sunny courtyard of his villa just outside Florence. His arthritis was bothering him. Perhaps he would feel better in the early October sunshine. He sat down carefully, and lovingly caressed the thick, leather-bound book in his hands. It was his latest work, called *Dialogue Concerning the Two Chief World Systems*. At long last, the book he had dreamed of writing! Seventeen years had passed since Cardinal Bellarmine had warned him not to "hold or defend" the Copernican system of the universe. So much had happened since then. Galileo had overcome many obstacles to make the book a reality.

In 1616 he had returned to Florence from Rome with all hopes for writing the book destroyed. For eight years he was silent, obeying the command delivered by Cardinal Bellarmine. He turned his attention to other problems in science involving motion and navigation. He had improved his telescope and had developed a simple microscope. Then in August 1623 came good news. His old friend Maffeo Barberini had become Pope Urban VIII. Galileo's spirits rose. Surely this ruler would be in favor of new ideas! With high hopes he went to Rome to seek permission to write his book.

Pope Urban welcomed him and spent many hours in conversation with his old friend. Finally, he gave Galileo the permission he wanted, but with reservations. First, Galileo must present the Copernican system as only an idea, not as a fact in reality. Second, Galileo must get Church approval of the manuscript before publishing the book. Galileo agreed happily to these conditions. Cardinal Bellarmine's old warning did not come up much in their conversations, since the new Pope wanted to establish his own authority. He also wanted his reign to be known for great works, and Galileo's book would show the world that the modern Church was not threatened by new ideas.

The writing turned out to be very slow work. Galileo wanted to be careful and thorough. He wrote the book as a conversation among three men. One character spoke for Galileo (and Copernicus). Another spoke for the traditional Ptolemaic view. His name was Simplicio, which meant "simple-minded." The third character was named Sagredo, after his old friend, who had died a few years earlier. In the book, Sagredo was an intelligent person with an open mind, as the real Sagredo had been. The purpose of the dialogue was to let Sagredo decide which system of the universe was correct. All the arguments for and against each system were presented. Though Galileo was fair in presenting both sides, no intelligent reader could have any doubt which side was correct. There was no denying that the Copernican system was simpler and more useful than the Ptolemaic for predicting the positions of the planets.

Galileo wrote the book in everyday Italian, rather than in Latin, the language of churchmen and scholars. Thus the book would be available to intelligent people in the public who were not connected with the Church or the universities. Still, Galileo did appear to follow the Pope's orders. At the end of the book, Simplicio (the character who spoke for Ptolemy) says that the Copernican system is simply an idea, one of many possibilities. But the arguments in favor of the Copernican system had been presented so powerfully that this small disclaimer was like closing the barn door after the horses had escaped.

After the writing, which took five years, came the problem of getting approval from the Church. Some of the official readers raised their eyebrows. They felt Galileo had only gone through the motions of obeying the Pope. Finally, however, approval for publication was granted. It was done. The first publication was in Florence, where Galileo had presented his patron, the Grand Duke, with a finished copy of the book seven months before. Then the book was published in Rome in June. It was an unexpected instant success. Copies disappeared from bookstores faster than they could be replaced.

Suddenly, without warning, trouble started. In August, Church officials removed all copies of the *Dialogue* from bookstores, and soon afterward the book was put on the Church list of banned books, so that reading or owning the book was a crime against the Church. Galileo was completely bewildered by this turn of events, but he did not know yet that Pope Urban had become his personal enemy. Apparently someone had convinced him that Galileo had used him as the model for Simplicio, the "simple-minded."

Galileo tenderly opened the book in his lap and leafed through the pages in the early autumn sunlight. So much pain and joy had gone into its creation! It was like a child to him, a child in trouble.

Suddenly his peace was disturbed by a servant.

"Signore Galileo, the Inquisitor of Florence is here to see you."

With a sinking feeling in the pit of his stomach Galileo said, "Show him in."

Galileo's old friend Father Stefani entered the courtyard. "It is with great regret, Galileo, that I perform my duty. On this day of October 1, 1632, I serve this official summons by the Inquisition in Rome. You have thirty days to journey to Rome to answer charges against you by the Inquisition."

The summons was more than Galileo could stand. It was so unjust! He was innocent! This he knew in the depths of his soul. He truly believed he had only told the truth in his book *with the Pope's approval*. The news was too much for him. He collapsed and had to be put to bed.

Friends wrote the Pope and anyone else who might have some influence. They explained that Galileo was almost seventy years old and very ill. They feared the 200-mile journey would kill him. But Pope Urban insisted. The Holy Father felt that Galileo had made a fool of him. After a few months' delay the Holy Office ordered Galileo to make the trip or else be brought to Rome in chains. In January 1633, Galileo slowly and painfully set off for Rome. To give him as much comfort as possible, the Grand Duke had loaned him his own coach for the trip.

In Rome, Galileo stayed at the home of the Tuscan ambassador, where he was treated with every kindness. Strangely, the Church didn't seem to be in a hurry to bring him to trial now that he was in Rome. Weeks went by. Galileo slowly regained his health and his fighting spirit. For the life of him he couldn't figure out why the Pope had turned against him. Deep in his heart he believed that he could still convince his old friend that his views were correct and that he had not committed a crime against the Church.

But Pope Urban VIII was very different from the Cardinal Barberini he had once been. His reign had truly changed him. He saw enemies everywhere. He even lived in a palace outside Rome with guards stationed along the road, because he feared he would be poisoned. It was hard for a reasonable person like Galileo to understand such unreasonable behavior in another.

In March, the Tuscan ambassador heard from the Pope that Galileo would soon be called to trial. Galileo was ready. He listened carefully as the ambassador reported to him about his visit with the Holy Father.

"The Pope told me that you had been his friend and that he was sorry that you had to suffer these troubles. But it is a matter of faith and religion. He said that it is not our job to decide how God does His work." Galileo leaned forward and stroked his beard.

"I thought you would be willing to say that you don't believe in the motion of the earth," the ambassador continued, "but that you would maintain, since God was all-powerful and could make the universe in a thousand different ways, that He could have made it his way, too, with the sun at its center. The Pope became furious at this statement, so I stopped saying anything that could hurt you. I feel it is very important that you obey him and do whatever he asks in the interest of religion."

Galileo nodded his agreement. But his eyes were sad.

Finally, in the middle of April, Galileo was transferred to the Inquisition headquarters and kept as a prisoner. He began a series of appearances before the ten judges of the Inquisition, where many questions were asked of him. Things began to close in when they brought up the subject of that meeting long ago with Cardinal Bellarmine:

"What did Cardinal Bellarmine tell you in February 1616?"

"He told me I was not to hold or defend the Copernican system."

Galileo produced a letter that Cardinal Bellarmine had written him after the spoken warning. It confirmed that Galileo was telling the truth.

"Who was present during this meeting?"

Suddenly Galileo was afraid.

"Some Dominican fathers. But I do not know their names and I haven't seen them since."

Galileo saw the danger. Cardinal Bellarmine was dead. He had no witnesses to that long ago confrontation.

Then came the cruelest blow of all. The Inquisitors produced a document dated at the time of that meeting. It was a formal warning from Bellarmine to Galileo. The language was much stronger than any Galileo remembered:

"Your opinion of the universe is wrong. You must forget it. You must not teach or defend it in any way whatsoever. If you do, you will have to answer to the Inquisition of the Holy Office."

Galileo was dumbfounded. Bellarmine had never told him he could not "teach" the Copernican system "in any way whatsoever." Clearly his book would be in violation of this order. The book did not violate Bellarmine's instructions as Galileo had understood them. In it he had only presented the Copernican view. But he personally had not "held" or "defended" it. There was no way he could now convince the Inquisition that he had not gone against the Pope's orders. Just to mention the Copernican system went against the order not to teach it "in any way whatsoever."

Where had this document come from? Galileo had never set eyes on it before. It was entirely possible that it was a forgery made by some of the present authorities who wanted to make sure of the case against him. If so, their trick had worked. Obviously the Pope was convinced that Galileo had committed a crime against the Church. Galileo had no proof on his side.

Galileo was defeated. The Inquisition found him guilty. Now came the painful wait for sentencing. They could do with him what they wished.

The Tuscan ambassador had some hope about the sentence. After all, Galileo was an old man and well respected. But the methods of the Inquisition were well known. If there were any resistance, if a prisoner clung to his forbidden beliefs, they simply used torture. The most common instrument of torture was the rack. They strapped a man to it and stretched him until his spine cracked and his muscles were torn apart. A younger man might survive it, but it would kill Galileo. Again the ambassador advised him to be quiet and obedient.

It was now the middle of June. For two months Galileo had been a prisoner. Although he had been treated well and allowed three rooms and a servant, the strain of being under lock and key showed.

On the morning of June 22 he was dressed in a coarse white robe and brought before the full court of the Inquisition. He now had little hope of being treated with mercy. The day before, the judges had asked:

"Do you or do you not believe in Copernicus?"

"No," answered Galileo, "not since before the warning in 1616."

"Doesn't your book, the *Dialogue*, support Copernicus?"

"No," answered Galileo. "I tried to show that neither Copernicus or Ptolemy are certain."

"Do you believe the earth moves?"

"No," answered Galileo. The judges had to lean forward to hear his answer. The old man in the rough clothing of a Church prisoner seemed to shrink before them. They did not see the tears in his eyes. They could not begin to understand the depths of his anguish.

"I am here to do whatever you want of me," the old man murmured.

And today he would find out what that was. He felt his public life to be over. There was no hope of convincing the Pope or the Church. His book was banned. He could not sink any lower in his own eyes. Now what? He knelt before his judges while they read the charges and the sentence.

Life imprisonment! But first he had to swear before the world that the truth—as he knew it—was false. He had to make a public denial, undoing all his work. His denial of the earth's movement in court the day before was not enough.

This was his greatest humiliation!

With a shaking hand Galileo wrote the document:

"I, Galileo, son of the late Vincenzo Galilei, aged seventy years . . . do swear that I have always believed . . . all that is taught and preached by the Holy Catholic Church. I wholly give up the false opinion that the sun is the center of the universe and does not move and the earth is not the center of the universe and moves. . . . I have abjured, sworn, and promised the truth of this document. . . ."

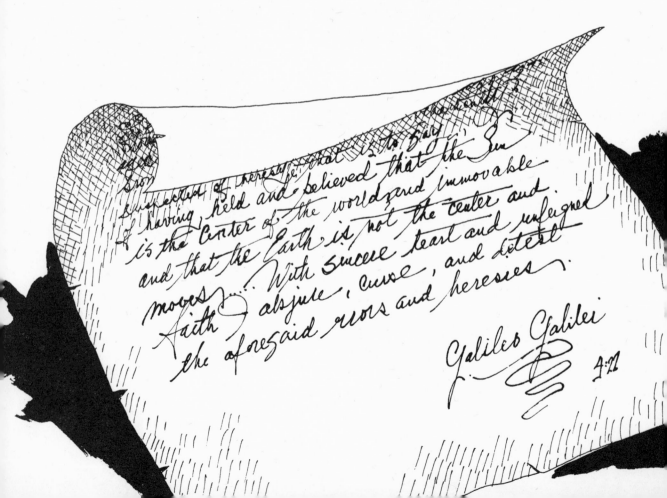

His life imprisonment turned out to be not such a heavy burden. He was allowed to return home to Florence, where his home was his prison. He wasn't allowed to leave. He spent the remaining eight years of his life writing a book on two new sciences, which became the beginning of modern physics. He played his lute and cultivated his olive trees. Always there was a steady stream of visitors.

There are some who feel that Galileo betrayed his beliefs, that he should have held fast and been burned at the stake. But Galileo was an intelligent man who saw through the men of the Church. He came to realize that the authorities were not interested in truth, only in their own power. By submitting he saved his own life. He knew that he had work of great value still to do.

And it was no secret to his many friends that Galileo believed to his dying day that the earth does in fact move around the sun and that it spins to create night and day. Galileo had absolute faith that, in the end, truth would be victorious.

SOME PEOPLE TO KNOW ABOUT

ARISTOTLE (384-322 B.C.)   Greek philosopher and natural scientist whose ideas became dominant in the late Middle Ages.

CARDINAL BELLARMINE (1542-1621)   Head of the College of Cardinals. Though he was open to new ideas, he warned Galileo about the danger of advocating his theory of the universe.

MAFFEO BARBERINI (1568-1644)   Became Pope Urban VIII in 1623. At first a liberal thinker, he became responsible for the conviction of Galileo by the Inquisition.

GIORDANO BRUNO (1548?-1600)   Italian philosopher and an early champion of the Copernican system of the universe.

NICOLAUS COPERNICUS (1473-1543)   Polish astronomer whose heliocentric model of the universe provided the basis of modern astronomy.

VINCENZO GALILEI (?-1591)   The father of Galileo. He was a lutenist, singer, writer and composer.

JOHANNES KEPLER (1571-1630)   German astronomer who established the laws governing the motions of the planets and who helped to establish the truth of the Copernican system.

HANS LIPPERSHEY (1587-1619)   A Dutch lens grinder who invented a telescope in 1608.

PTOLEMY (2nd century A.D.)   Egyptian astronomer whose geocentric model of the universe was widely accepted in the late Middle Ages.

EVANGELISTA TORRICELLI (1608-1647)   A student of Galileo who later established the existence of atmospheric pressure, invented the mercury barometer, and made many other important discoveries in physics and mathematics.

GIOSEFFO ZARLINO (1517-1590)   Franciscan monk who made important contributions to musical theory.

SELECTED BIBLIOGRAPHY

Boas, Marie. *The Scientific Renaissance* 1450-1630. New York: Harper & Row, 1962.

Bolton, Sarah K. *Famous Men of Science*. New York: Thomas Y. Crowell Company, 1960.

Brecht, Bertolt. *Galileo, A Play*. New York: Grove Press, 1966.

De Santillana, Giorgio. *The Crime of Galileo*. Chicago: The University of Chicago Press, 1955.

Fermi, Laura and Gilberto Bernardini. *Galileo and the Scientific Revolution*. New York: Basic Books, Inc., 1961.

Galilei, Galileo. *Dialogue Concerning The Two Chief World Systems*. Berkeley: University of California Press, 1953.

Ronan, Colin A. *Galileo*. New York: G.P. Putnam's Sons, 1974.

Severy, Merle, ed. *The Renaissance: Maker of Modern Man*. National Geographic Society, 1970.

Smith, A.G.R. *Science & Society in the Sixteenth and Seventeenth Centuries*. New York: Science History Publications, 1972.

VICKI COBB is the author of several books for young people, including *Science Experiments You Can Eat* and *How the Doctor Knows You're Fine*. She has also created filmstrips and other educational aids and has written scripts for network television.

Ms. Cobb, a resident of Mamaroneck, New York, holds degrees from Barnard College and Columbia University Teachers College.

GEORGE ULRICH was born in Morristown, New Jersey, and received his B.F.A. degree from Syracuse University School of Art. He has illustrated many educational texts and trade books, including Nancy Veglahn's *Dance of the Planets: The Universe of Nicolaus Copernicus*, published by Coward, McCann & Geoghegan.

Mr. Ulrich lives with his wife and their two children in Marblehead, Massachusetts.